Unlocking God's Plans for

Your Life

Timothy Wright

ISBN 978-1-64416-081-7 (paperback)
ISBN 978-1-64416-082-4 (digital)

Christian Faith Publishing, Inc.
832 Park Avenue
Meadville, PA 16335
www.christianfaithpublishing.com

Printed in the United States of America

About the Title

Looking back, I can see God's hand in my frustration with trying to share my faith. Most of the poems in this book were written at a time when I just didn't know what else to do … but God did. I had a desire to witness for the Lord and share my faith but felt that when I did, the words I really wanted to share were not there. So I began to write poems and found I was able to say the things God wanted me to say with poetry. *Unlocking God's Plans for Your Life* will bring the reader face-to-face with the question: do I really know Jesus? Every poem has a different way to bring them to this question and pleads with the reader to search his or her heart, to unlock God's plans for their life. This would be a book you might want to use to share your faith with someone and help them unlock God's plans for their life.

Contents

Filled to Overflowing

Do you know God knows all your thoughts? Believe it or not, it's true.
All your dreams, all your fears, and everything you do.
You can tell God all your secret things you would never share.
He puts them in the sea of forgetfulness, and He says no fishing here.
You say there's sins you won't give up … sins you like to do.
With God, you really don't give up … you trade for something new.
When I gave to Him my pennies, He was very generous you see.
I reached inside my pockets … gold coins were given me.
He satisfied the hungry heart with more than it could hold.
And filled it up way past the top until it overflowed.
So bring to Him your deepest hurts and see what He will do.
And also sins you struggle with … He even takes them, too.
Bring your questions, bring your doubts, bring Him everything.
I challenge you to bring them all till there's nothing more to bring.
Beyond your dreams, beyond your hopes, beyond what you've been told.
There is a love God pours in us … our hearts could never hold.

Jesus Was More Messed Up Than You

Do you think you could never be a Christian because your life is such a mess?

God fixes messed-up people ... let's put Him to the test.

You might have tried it once before, but did you understand? You can't do this on your own ... you need to trust in Him.

Just come to Jesus as you are ... that always works the best. He's the One who does the work and cleans up all the mess.

If you think you don't need His help, you better think again. Because pride can keep you far away ... and that's a bigger sin.

So why not try it one more time ... you can start today. The cross is where you need to go ... it's the only way.

Yes, the cross is where you must begin ... it will help you with your pride. You need to see how He suffered and was rejected before He died.

You can put a cross around your neck or hang it on a wall, but until you've been to Calvary, it has no power at all.

Paint it on your body or put it on your arm, but just remember this, my friend ... it's not a good luck charm.

His road to Calvary was painful ... every step was out of love. He was weak from all the beatings as He left a trail of blood.

When Calvary's hill He had to climb, He had my sins and yours in mind. Out of strength but not out of love ... even forsaken by His Father above.

So don't tell me you're so messed up, that you can't try again. Jesus was more messed up than you when all our sins were put on Him.

Secure in Christ

Has He not chosen you … you didn't choose Him.

And did He not count the cost when He paid off all your sin.

So why are you surprised when He looks inside of you?

And shows you things that are in your heart … things you never knew.

God is living in you … that's always been His plan.

It's what He meant when He said to you, "You must be born again."

There's something deeper going on … it's like a marriage that seals the bond.

He's gone too far to turn back now … He's made the seal, He's vowed the vow.

Nothing can separate Him from you … not a demon from hell or things you do.

The cross sealed our bond. You need to understand.

The cords that were tied were tied by His own hand.

He's not a man that He could lie … His cords are strong; His bond is tied.

He lost us once, but never again. The cross has brought us back to Him.

Could He love you more … I see no way. He poured His love on you that day.

With thicker cords of mercy and grace, His blood poured out, our sins erased.

So if you wonder how secure you really are … let me tell you once again.

No power from Heaven or of hell below could take you from His hand.

Returning Home

Has your journey been long? Has it caused your heart to roam?
Are you lost and confused and a long way from home?
It's never too late, no matter where you've been.
The Father's always waiting to bring you back to him.
We've all been down that road. Don't think you're all alone.
You need to make another turn and take the road back home.
The road that you are on, you will never find the end.
It goes around and turns around and brings you back again.
Take the road less traveled and it will lead you home.
You'll know when you are on it … your heart will no more roam.
We'll all be there to greet you when you make your final turn.
Just don't look back and don't turn back to lessons you have learned.
Life is full of choices … sometimes, the bad ones we will do.
But our God is a great redeemer … He makes beauty from this too.
So if your journey has left you lost and burdened down with sin.
You could start your journey home that leads you back to him.
If you take one step, the Father will take two.
But the first step is the hard step … that step is up to you.

The Doorway to My Heart

I know the struggles in your life … I can feel your pain.
Don't forget my love for you … come near to Me again.
I am not a fairy tale or a wish upon a star.
But everything you need in life … I am near to you, not far.
I formed you in your mother's womb and watched you struggle in
    the night.
I long for you to trust in me and make me your delight!
There's a doorway to my heart … a key that you must find.
It unlocks your heart to me and makes you only mine.
Take my hand and follow Me … I will guide the way.
Through life's storms, hold tight to Me, and I will be your stay.
The peace that I have for you is greater than your fears.
There are no boundaries to my love … always endless through the years.
Look for Me in everything as you go throughout your day.
Without Me, you are not complete … I made you just that way.
When I designed your heart, there's something you should know,
I left for Me the biggest part … that's so my love can grow.
The cross will open a door for you and unlock your love for Me.
It is the doorway to my heart … just try the key and see.

Don't Forget Who You Are

When you're faced with an enemy that's bigger than you, some say
that surrendering is all you can do.
Or if the mountain before you looks too big to climb, the same peo-
ple will tell you you're wasting your time.
Unless you know the One who put the mountain there, you'll walk
away defeated … all those voices you will hear.
Have you forgotten who you are? Let me tell you once again. You're
a child of God, sons and daughters of Him.
This mountain before you is not too big, when the One who made
it inside you lives.
Defeat is not an option with God's sword in your hand. Your enemy
will bow down at the voice of your command.
A victory cry went out when Jesus died on that cross. "It is finished"
is still sounding … Satan knows the battle's lost.
Even death has been defeated … there's no temptation you can't bear.
You see, the stone's been rolled away and His body isn't there.

New Beginnings

If your life is filled with mistakes ... I wish I would have and what I should have done. You could be a candidate for a second chance ... a new beginning ... a brand-new one.

If you're living in your past, there's nothing there you can change. But if you want to change your future, you need to stop and rearrange.

Maybe start with your priorities ... let's make God number 1. You can't pretend He knows your heart ... before you start, this must be done.

Remember, you're getting a new beginning ... you get to start all over again. It might be hard, but it will be worth it ... new beginnings have better ends.

You really have nothing to lose ... other than mistakes and lots of pain. So why not do it God's way ... your mistakes, He turns to gain.

Now a battle will begin ... it's a battle for control. But you're the only one who's fighting ... you could trust God and just let go.

Because whoever wins this battle will determine your destiny. Old ways are hard to break ... but new beginnings can set you free.

So if you're tired of your old ways, why not try something new? It's too late to change your past, but not too late to change you.

Author and producer of new beginnings ... the Holy Spirit co-starring God the Father and Jesus the Son.

P.S. New beginnings are not for everyone ... only for those who are willing to come.

To You Who Will Listen

To you who are hurting now, give me your ears, and I'll tell you a story passed down through the years.

The story's unending … the message still true. Pay attention, my friend … this could be for you.

This is a story the proud will not hear, but you who are hurting … come now and draw near.

Pain is God's phone … is He calling today? Are you going through life, but not looking His way?

So for you who are hurting, this could be God's test. He says, "Come to Me, and I'll give you rest."

This story is repeated down through the years, when we cry out to God, He really hears.

But those who are proud will go their own way. "That's for the weak … not for me," they will say.

It is for the weak, but with God, we're made strong. I'd rather be weak and be right and not wrong.

To you who will love Him, this message is clear; we find that through suffering, our hearts are drawn near.

To you who are proud this does not apply … but neither will grace on the day that you die.

Free Indeed

Jesus heals from inside out ... do you need His touch today?

We're not born broken people ... we just get broken along the way.

Because we all have broken dreams and broken dreams make broken hearts.

Did you know your Maker sees the crack before it even starts?

Only He's the Great Physician ... only He was without sin.

Only He knows where to touch you and make you whole again.

If life has left you broken and also left you pain,

I have good news you need to hear ... there's help in Jesus's name!

The first step is the hardest ... just walk, don't try to run.

But when you feel Him, take your hand, your healing has begun.

By now your outside's doing good, but your inside needs more time.

Because He heals from inside out, when He's done, you'll do just fine.

Now if you were to do nothing to try and stop this pain,

His power inside you dwindles and your life begins to drain.

All the dreams that could have been ... one by one they too will end.

There will be bumps along the way ... but his grace is all you'll need.

If you continue, you'll hear Him say, "Who the Son sets free is free indeed!"

God's Handiwork

Every day should be a day God shows us something new. Yes, every day something new ... that's not too hard for God to do.

He makes every snowflake ... not two of them the same. Warms them up, if He gets bored and turns them into rain.

He's full of new ideas He wants to share with you and me. He loves it when we're overwhelmed with everything we see.

So if you think God is boring and that He's just no fun, go take a walk on a starry night and see what He has done.

Heaven is just His handiwork, but we're the apple of His eye. Did you know He loves us more than all the stars in the sky?

God won't force His love on you ... that's not what He would do. He proved His love on Calvary ... now the choice is up to you.

How can you go through life even though He's everywhere, pretend that you don't see Him and pretend he doesn't care.

And what do you do with Jesus who gave His life for you? Will you turn your head and walk away and say it isn't true?

Because then, every sunset will never be the same. The Master painted it just for you ... that would be a shame.

So this is my suggestion to what you should do ... Give Him the canvass of your life and let Him repaint you.

Thank God Our God Is a Jealous God!

What if the plans God has for you are not what you would choose?
And all the dreams of your heart, one by one, you would lose.
Then this could be the message you need to hear today.
Did you know life can get better when things don't go your way?
Because what if every dream you had would suddenly come true,
And it made you sad instead of happy … then what would you do?
God knows this world can take our hearts and steal our love away.
So instead of being mad … try thanking Him today.
Maybe your broken dreams are a sign of what real love will do.
When God sees the things in your heart, He is jealous over you.
He didn't just create you and say, "Go and do your thing."
He had a plan … He had a purpose … in His heart, He had a dream.
Will you run from Him? Where would you go?
There's no place you can hide.
And even if you found a place, you would have no peace inside.
So be glad your God is a jealous God when you don't get your way,
Remember your heart means more to Him than the things you
    get today.

How Much Will You Give?

Why did God send His Son … this is something you need to know.
Without this truth, your faith is dead and won't begin to grow.
Some will hear, but they will not understand. Others will hear, and
they will turn
to Him. So what made the difference? Doesn't God love us all?
The difference is this … some will answer His call. God tells us many
times there's
just one way to start. If you hear Him calling, harden not your heart.
Some, when He calls, will close their ear. Others will listen, and He
draws them
near. Some try to find him by using their mind.
Others are always looking for some kind of sign. But God is a God
who searches
our hearts. When we find Him there, that's where He starts.
Some will give up everything. They will love Him that much.
Others won't give Him the time of day … they say He's just a crutch.
So the choice is really up to you, to be wise in life or to be a fool.
But the outcome will not be the same, you can live forever or die in vain?

New Job

So who wants to be a servant … can I see a show of hands?
I need someone to put others first … if that's you and you think you can.
The pay's not very good, but the benefits can't be beat.
Your trainer will be Jesus … he's free, but he's not cheap.
Forget about your old life, and join the Jesus team.
Get ready for your new life; it's beyond your wildest dream!
The things in life you used to do; they just won't seem the same.
Jesus is your new boss now; there's things he'll want to change.
Little by little you'll trust him more, and learn to just let go.
Then one day, he'll take the wheel and you'll give Him full control.
When Jesus is in control, there are things you begin to say.
I used to really love to do this, but the desire has gone away.
He fills our life with so much more … it's easy to just let go.
Because in your heart, you found a peace you never thought you'd know.
So if you want to serve a king, God's taking applications today.
You can challenge yourself and still be yourself … God takes you just
    that way.

Just Imagine

Just imagine you're not in Heaven because Jesus Christ was not
    your Lord;
In your life, you did it your way; you tried Him once but you were bored.
Many times, God tried to call you, but in your heart, you turned away.
Friends and loved ones tried to warn you; "That works for you" is
    what you'd say.
Now your time on earth has ended; every chance you had is gone.
You stand before Him empty-handed and realize that you were wrong.
Right now, there's hope because you're still living; one more chance
    you get today.
God's calling everyone to serve Him, most will turn and walk away.
You could delete or trash this message, or you could rise up to His call.
"Become a warrior in God's army," then stand before Him proud
    and tall.

Passport to Heaven

If we compare ourselves with others, we will never see our sin.
We'll always find someone and say, "Well, I'm not as bad as him."
Did you know that pride is a deceiver … it tells us things that just
    aren't true.
Now I'm not that bad at all when I compare myself to you.
So compare yourself to Jesus … then tell me where you stand.
I'll tell you now what I found out … I was a wretched man.
God's grace is free to everyone who's trusting in the cross.
To our serial killers in prison and to our heroes at war we lost.
Yes, even our prisoners go free when they put their trust in him.
But those free without Christ are more bound up than them.
There's only one passport to Heaven … all others will be denied.
If your hope is not in Jesus, you're believing Satan's lie.
You think you're a pretty good person, and your good will outweigh
    your bad.
You better think twice before you roll those dice,
Because snake eyes is what you have.
So when you die and stand before God, just remember one thing …
God will look at you and then your passport … it better say "Redeemed."

Sharing Our Faith

Lord, how do I share my faith with others?
I've told them you're the bridge over troubled waters.
I've asked them if they were to die, where would they be today?
I've even told them you alone are the only way.
They don't really hang around too long; so I wonder, Lord, am I
    doing it wrong?
Are people just too busy to spend time with you?
If they knew what they were missing, it would be all they'd want to do.
When they seek you, they will find you because you're never far away.
If they could only see your glory, then I know they'd want to stay.
Now I'm running out of things to do; is there a better way to tell
    them about you?
And I'm running out of things to say; there's got to be a different way.
I could write a poem, yes, that's what I'll do … but I can do nothing,
    Lord, without
You.
I can put it on paper and pray they'll read … if you'll open their eyes
and give them faith to believe.

Do You Have the Right Jesus?

Do you have the real Jesus? I pray to God you do.
Because there's a lot of them around, but only One is really true.
Does He have your heart and are you trusting in Him?
Is He Lord of your life, or is He just a good friend.
The real Jesus has a cross He gives to me and you.
And on that cross, He showed the world what real love would do.
The heavens were watching on that day as darkness filled the air.
You know, it wasn't just the nails that held Him up there.
Our debt was so great, it took his blood to pay the cost.
Did you know that it was love that held Him to the cross?
So do you have the right Jesus … the one who died to set you free?
The one all heaven's eyes were watching when they nailed Him to
   that tree.
He could have called ten thousand angels to take Him from that cross.
But don't you know if He did that, we would still be lost.
So if you have the right Jesus, there's a cross you bear today.
And that cross to you is precious because it took your sins away.
So have you found the real Jesus … there's only one in all the land.
You'll know Him when you find Him … He has a nail print in
   His hand.

Indescribable God

You can't put God in a picture frame; he's not at all like this. He's way too big for your fireplace, and there's a lot you're going to miss.

He's a God of love and a God of war and a God of peace and so much more. He holds yesterday, today, and forever in his hands.

With our little minds, we could never understand. His attributes are innumerable; his ways past finding out.

He's the Lord of lords and King of kings; if you've ever had a doubt. He always was and always will be eternal and forever, God Almighty.

The Alpha and Omega ... the beginning and the end; The Creator and sustainer. All things come from him.

I hope you're getting the picture. He's really big, you see. He holds the universe in his hands; he's not like you and me.

The earth is just his footstool and the heavens are his throne. But what makes him even bigger yet, our hearts he calls his home.

And out of all of his creation, the cross cannot compare. He redeems lost sinners like you and me and he does it all right there.

You see ... when he created the heavens and laid out all its plans, He forgot just one thing ... He forgot all of your sins.

That's when mercy left a trail for all of us to see; it started at the heart of God and stopped ... at Calvary.

Have you found that trail, my friend? It continues to this day. It's going to take you to the cross ... and wash your sins away.

Sowing Seeds

You say you got excited once; you even shed a tear;
The Word of God touched your heart ... that's really nice to hear.
Jesus talked about a farmer who sowed seeds along the way.
Some fell on rocks, other fell in thorns; the birds took some away.
But some also fell on good ground ... what's Jesus trying to say?
The Word of God is like a seed ... to make it grow, there's things
    you need.
A listening ear and believing heart can give this seed a perfect start.
So why all the fuss with this little seed? In God's great wisdom, He
    made a plan
That with the foolishness of preaching, He would save man.
To those who won't seek Him with all their heart; the seed of faith
    won't even start.
So if the cares of this world is where your heart is found; your seed
probably landed on stony ground.
Or if God's Word really means nothing to you, it's probably choked
    out with all
the things that you do.
So let me help you if I can ... to see what went wrong, take a good
    look within.

No Ruts Too Deep

Do you want to grow old and be stuck in a rut?
Is that where your life's going to end?
You could go to the One who would set you free.
Now that's where your life could begin.
You don't want to be like a bird in a cage that never knew he could fly.
There were trees he could live in and winds he could soar
And rainbows to see in the sky.
Heaven help us, I pray, if we end up that way and miss the life God
    has planned.
So kick open that door and get out of that cage and fly like a bird in
    the wind.
There are songs to be sung and work to be done that only you can do.
The rut is the place where you'll see His grace ... look up; He'll res-
    cue you.
Life will get better; things will get brighter when you put your hope
    in Him.
He takes all of our ruts and buries them up to make sure that we
    don't fall in.
When I'm stuck in a rut, don't feel sorry for me; there's only one
    thing I can do.
I will look to the One who can set me free ... He will do the same
    for you.
So if you're stuck in a rut, don't stay in your rut ... I'm going to say
    it again.
If you live for yourself, you will die in your rut, so why not just live
    for Him?

Just a Sinner Saved by Grace

Did you know you're a bigger sinner than you even think you are?
But did you also know that you are loved by a much greater love by far.
Now I'm not trying to judge you … that's not where I'm going here.
I've learned this truth the hard way … by looking in the mirror.
The more I get to know Him, the more it's plain to see.
If it wasn't for His amazing grace … oh, Lord, where would we be?
So don't think your sin's so big you can't go to Him.
He loves big sinners by the way … I know … I'm one of them.
Forgiveness is what God does when He's reaching out his hand.
Even though we miss his mark, He says, "Come on, let's start again."
Jesus came to save sinners just like you and me.
If you think you're not a sinner, then you're blind and you can't see.
I can still remember the day and will never forget the night
When I asked Jesus in my heart and He gave me back my sight.
He has never ever left me from that very moment on.
I'm not perfect just forgiven … yes, every sin is gone.
Oh, His precious love … it reaches down to where we are.
So don't even think you're beyond his reach … you could never go
     that far.

The Big House

There's more to life than what our eyes can see, and there's more to God than what our dreams could ever dream.

One day, you could wake up and be walking streets of gold, and up ahead, you'll see a crystal sea around God's royal throne.

Now I'm not talking about Disneyland or a place called make-believe. I'm talking about God's house ... it's way bigger than you ever dreamed!

It's 1,500 miles square and it's coming down from the sky, and even though it is so big, you could miss it when you die.

Now I don't claim to have been there or to have walked the streets of gold. But the One who tells the story ... He's the builder, I am told.

The walls are made of jasper ... it's beyond your wildest dream. This was not some ordinary house ... this is a palace for the King.

God revealed this vision to John, to him he would not hide; it was dazzling white ... so beautiful ... looking like a bride.

When you enter into this house, there is no need for light. No sun or moon will shine in it ... God's glory is so bright!

This is more like a city ... it has three gates on each side. And every gate had one pearl ... so big it could open wide.

But there was one more thing that John did see, and this one thing really bothered me. There were lots of loved ones that did not make it there,

But God himself was wiping away everybody's tears. Heaven's not a fairy tale ... every word of God is true.

But when your loved ones get to Heaven, will God be wiping their tears for you?

What Will the Verdict Be?

Did you hear the story of the little boy who was saved when his house burnt down?

He lost everything … his mom and his dad; he had no family around.

The people felt bad … they were fighting for him. The judge didn't know what to do. Then a stranger came in and said, "I'll take him." He was someone that nobody knew.

The judge was amazed as he looked at the man. "What gives you the right to him?"

Then he showed him his hands … they were burnt from the fire. He said, "I was the one who went in."

The courtroom was cleared … this case is through. The stranger that saved him … this child goes to you.

Now Jesus didn't save you from a burning fire, but He can save you from the fires of hell.

And there is a fight about who's going get you … either Satan or Immanuel.

There won't be a judge or even a jury … only you can decide this case.

Jesus was nailed to a cross … He has scars in His hands … on that cross He took your place.

Satan will trick you … Jesus will love you. Don't be deceived, my friend.

It's Heaven or hell … the choice is still yours. The verdict will come in the end.

So how could you doubt that Jesus loves you … the answer is so plain to me.

The question is now, do you love Jesus … when the verdict comes in, we will see.

God So Loved the World

So what are you going to do with Jesus? Is he just a legend from times
  of old?
Did you know he said he was God … now that was pretty bold.
He was either the biggest liar the world has ever seen, or was he God
  like he said he was … this often troubled me.
Did he know what he was saying … had he gone off the deep end?
  He said that he was God; I Am … the great I Am.
That's why they crucified him … they hung him on a tree. But death
  couldn't keep him in the ground, because he was God, you see.
Sin had entered into the world and it passed from man to man. So
  all creation was under sin till the cross when God stepped in.
It was love that kept him on the cross; his love for you and me. Till
  the power of sin was broken, and he paid your penalty.
Because God changes everything; that's what his love can do. We are
  broken people in a broken world, but he can make us new.
Jesus had to come into the world to break the power of sin. Time
  stood still, erased itself, and started over again.
We went from BC to AD. Did you ever think about that? Over two
  thousand years ago, God did something new.
He erased everything and started again; He can do the same for you.

Finding True Love

Did you take a chance with love, and once again, it broke your heart?
You really want to love again, but too afraid to start.
You can search the deepest ocean or look beyond the stars above.
But I've discovered a different way that guarantees you love.
The kind of love you're looking for is really very near.
It always was and always is … no farther than a prayer.
Give your heart to Jesus … put your trust in Him.
He heals the brokenhearted so they can love again.
He picks up broken pieces of lives along the way;
And binds them up and heals them up … do you need His help today?
And when you're feeling lonely like the times you did before;
He gives you peace you never had and makes you love Him more.
I just thought I needed to tell you about how much He loves you so.
The choice is really up to you, but I wanted you to know.
So now if you reject Him like many people do,
It must be you don't love Him as much as He loves you.

I've Been to the Woodshed

You have taught me, Lord, to fear your name.
Life's trials and consequences have brought much pain.
I've been to the woodshed again and again.
Your ways are better … I have learned firsthand.
Our hearts are only content if we are following You.
We deceive ourselves if we think it's not true.
Sometimes, we believe that we know right from wrong.
The real truth is we are weak and not strong.
But our God is faithful … He is loving and kind.
He says, "When I correct you, it's because you are mine."
His Word is hard I will not say.
There's joy in this journey when I follow His way.
Your path on earth will bind us and when death knocks on our door.
His love will surely find us and we will suffer no more.
Until that day, He'll keep us … He cannot deny His name.
If we cling to the cross of Jesus, our suffering's not in vain.
So if the woodshed's what it takes to make our hearts be true,
We will gladly take a beating, Lord, if it brings us back to you.

Time to Choose

So you really think that you can overcome sin when your flesh cries
out, "Let's do it again."

Satan sets his traps with lust and greed; he'll choose his bait to fit
your needs.

You're no match against sin, now there's no doubt. It'll chew you up
and spit you out.

You say you're strong willed; now that won't do; he's got lots of tricks
for those like you.

"But I'm a good person, I don't even sin"; that's a big lie if you're not
born again. He says if your hand sins to cut it off,

And if your eye sins, to gouge it out. Now those are strong words
without a doubt; but our flesh is strong and it's prone to sin,

And it will take a strong word and God's grace to win. There's only
one way before God we can stand; it's in the power of his cross
and the blood of the lamb.

So let's get one thing perfectly clear: This world's not your home;
don't get comfortable here.

Sin's fun for a season … we know it's true; but God's love lasts for-
ever; that's a lot to lose.

God's grace is free … it's not cheap, you see; you can't live in sin and
call God your friend.

Live for him or live for you … think it out; think it through. The
results will be forever; now the choice is up to you.

Only One Way

Is God really mean? That's what people say. You'll all burn in Hell if you don't do it His way.

Wait a minute here … let's think this thing through. Is God really mean … is He really that cruel?

If you're on a sinking ship and you hear the captain say, "Everyone to a lifeboat … it's our only way."

Would you think that he was mean or that he doesn't even care? No, you would get into the lifeboat … it would be your only prayer.

This world's a sinking ship … going deeper into sin. Jesus is our lifeboat … are you on board with Him?

At the click of a mouse, you can go places you don't want to be. Going deeper and deeper into sin … there's no bottom to that sea.

There's only one way up … I can tell you what to do. Get into the lifeboat … it can rescue you.

When Jesus was in the garden, He cried out, "Is there another way?" Heaven was silent … not a word did the Father say.

He went from the garden to a rugged cross, there on Calvary He bled and died for sinners just like us.

Because God so loved the world that He gave His only Son, so if you're looking for another way … trust me, you won't find one.

The Greatest Story Never Told

Do you read your Bible? Do you know what it's about? Maybe it's time you stopped and took some time to check it out.

Just imagine there's a God who created all you see. And that He is a God of love so He created you and me.

He wrote a book to tell his story so all creation could see his glory. Then his children did something very hard to believe.

All the things that He created, they began to worship these. And the Bible that He gave them that told of all his glory;

They refused to believe it and made up a different story. His creation screams out, "I'm a very big God!"

But his children took trees and made their God out of these. They began to worship the god of their hands and soon forgot the God who made them.

They built houses and boats and played with their games and said to themselves, "Nothing has changed."

Things that ever were and ever will be; they all stay the same … it's just you and me. So the greatest story of the God of old was hardly even ever told.

Yes, they forgot God, and when death knocks on their door, they'll stand before the One they were created for.

Won't they be surprised … they thought He was dead. Would you please open your Bible to find out what God said.

God's Rest

As I go throughout my day, I see empty faces along the way. Then I stop to understand; there is no peace without Him.

I see them laughing when they're on their phone, but do you ever watch them when they're all alone?

I go to prison and they tell me there … when the lights go out is when people fear.

So at night when you go to bed, do you have peace with Jesus or is there fear instead? Because perfect love will cast out fear … have you ever asked Jesus to help you here?

Fear has torment that's not from above. Stay close to Jesus; there's power in His love. Just remember you're in a real war; that's what all your armor's for.

This war is of a different kind. You'll need God's helmet for your mind. When you trust Jesus as your Lord, the Word of God becomes your sword.

Your eyes will be open and then you'll know … that Satan is your real foe. Your enemy hides in dark places; that's why you fear. You'll need to just get out of there.

Satan's spirits are weary and they're searching for rest. If you hang out in dark places, you're a perfect nest. To come out from among them, you'll need your shield. Satan has no power when to faith you yield.

You'll also have freedom of a different kind; God's Word living in you will control your mind. The peace that you feel, you won't understand. But when the lights go out, you'll sleep again.

Win the Race

So how many sins did He forgive? Do you count them one by one?
Do you sort them out from big to small … don't you know He
takes them all.

You are in a race, my friend. You won't go anywhere carrying them.
If you're not saved by grace alone, then you're not saved at all.

Relax, it's Him that does the work … you just took the call. Every sin
you've ever done and all the sins that lie ahead … if you're going
to try to run this race, you need to give to Him.

When you see how much He cares for you and how He loves you so,
you will learn to run from sin … as fast as you can go.

It's His mercy and His truth that sets you free from sin. Sin won't
even have a chance when you make friends with them.

So forget about your old life, a new life you must choose. When you've
been chosen by God Himself, there's nothing you will lose.

This is how you overcome and learn to walk with Him. Once you
know the Father's love, His kindness takes you in.

Then sin will lose its grip on you and death will flee away. Come on,
what are you waiting for … if you're not saved today?

All good things come from above in case you didn't know. The best
things God has saved for us … and those who love Him so.

A Father's Love

Since the beginning of time till time is no more, God goes after and
God goes before.

He always was and He always will be the first and the last … God
Almighty.

So if you're struggling in life, why not go to Him? He's bigger and
wiser from beginning to end.

Don't just go through life feeling lost every day when your heavenly
Father says, "I am the way."

He sees all the struggles and pain you've been in. He waits at your
door and He's knocking again.

You can't just ignore Him … He's been there before. Maybe it's time
that you opened the door.

Your problems in life will not just go away, if you're running from
God and He's calling today.

So open your heart and just let Him in. He's been patiently waiting
again and again.

The one your heart longs for has been longing for you. When you
turn Him away, it hurts his heart too.

So where can you run and why would you go from your Heavenly
Father who loves you so?

His doorway is open … go quickly to Him. He's calling lost chil-
dren … it's time to come in.

Is It Time for a Tune-Up?

If your prayer life's almost gone and you're barely hanging on, you might need a resurrection ... not from the grave, but from beyond.

Jesus came to give us life and give it abundantly, so something's wrong if you don't have it ... let's take a look and see.

Did you know that repairing people is a lot like fixing a car? If a wire's bad, you could lose your spark ... you're not going very far.

Mechanics use a flashlight ... God's word can light our way. They fix things on their back ... we get on our knees and pray.

Now when I'm abiding in Him and His word is abiding in me, if I lose my spark or something's wrong, His word can help me see.

But if I forget my first love and go back to my old ways, then I forgot the blood He shed and the price He had to pay.

God has given us every tool to conquer the power of sin; but now and then we need a tune-up to help us live for Him.

Are you in need of a tune-up? Don't wait to call ahead. If you wait too long, you're going to need a tow truck instead!

One day, we'll stand before Him and see Him face-to-face, not clothed in our own righteousness, but in His amazing grace.

Until that day, Lord, help us to present ourselves to you, a vessel that has honored you in everything we do.

To You Who Are Hurting

In quietness and confidence you'll find your strength in Me.
When life gets rough, don't forget that I can calm the sea.
When the storms of life are all around and it's getting hard to stand,
Let Me be your anchor because I can still the wind.
I sometimes allow your enemies to cause you a little pain,
Because I know when I deliver you, you'll cling to Me again.
I saw you on that day when you surrendered your life to Me.
Not one moment have I left your side … every hair on your head I see.
So when your world around you goes upside down again,
Trust in Me with all your heart. Reach out … you'll find My hand.
For I have chosen you … you have not chosen Me.
You are the apple of my eye. All your struggles I do see.
You might not understand every trial that comes your way;
But remember this … I am the potter, and you, my child, the clay.
One day soon, you will look back and it will be plain to see.
With every trial you went through, you're looking more like Me.

How Can I Start Over?

If you really want to start over, today can be your day.
But all the mistakes you made in life, you can't just wipe away.
I don't think starting over means moving to another town.
Because all the baggage that you have just follows you around.
Jesus has a better way of starting over again.
Just take one day at a time as you learn to walk with Him.
Now about that baggage you collected through all the years.
It's time to lay it at the cross … every sorrow, every tear.
Let Jesus take that load … lay it down and walk away.
Don't look back or pick it up … today's a brand-new day.
This one thing will happen as you leave it at the cross … When you
    walk away,
you realize the pain is all you lost.
Now you're almost ready to start your life again.
Just don't go back or begin to think of how life could have been.
My prayer for you is one day soon, you'll get your brand-new start.
But don't forget, it must begin with Jesus in your heart.
I leave you now with one more tip on how you should begin …
Give it all to Jesus and you'll have a happy end.

A Real Friend

Everyone wants a real friend that will always be there.
They'd know your thoughts and know your dreams and always seem
    to care.
And when things in life would bring you down, they could cheer you
    up just being around.
When life gets hard and you get burned out, they're always there to
    help you out.
Isn't this the friend our hearts long for? The kind of friend you want
    to see at
your front door.
But the truth is with people, they can let us down. And sometimes
    the ones that
hurt us the most can be the ones that were so close.
Now there is a friend that is closer than a brother ... you have the
    same Father, but you don't have the same mother.
He is a friend that knows just what you need. His name is Jesus ...
    He's a friend
indeed.
I found something in Him I never found before. Then I realized He
    was the friend I was really looking for.
There were times I turned my back on Him, and I know I hurt Him so.
But He did something different then ... He would not let me go.
Then I knew He was the kind of friend that would love me always
    to the end.

Take Time for Him Today

God doesn't always call … you should be quick to let Him in.
Because if you don't, you might find out He won't be back again.
If He's tugging at your heart and all that you can say,
Is "I really don't have time right now … come back another day."
Or maybe you only go to God when you think life isn't fair.
Where were you God when I needed You … are You really even there?
God is like a friendship … it doesn't work just one way.
If you spend time with Him, He'll spend time with you as you go
     throughout your day.
But if you refuse to serve Him and follow His plan, why would you
     think that God would hear when you pray to Him?
There comes a time when God stops calling and He will turn and
     walk away.
So don't just think He's always there … your last call could be today.
The fear of the Lord is the beginning of wisdom … that's what the
     good book says.
But if you don't fear Him, you won't serve Him … that's just the
     way it is.

Heaven's Door

If your life is filled with stress, I know a quiet place to go,
If your grief is overwhelming and your joy is running low.
When you're there, you will discover His love can calm your fear,
It's a place unlike no other … not far away but very near.
The first time I went, I prayed, "O Lord, just let me stay,"
I have never felt the kind of peace that could take me through my day.
Many years have passed and now I go there even more,
One day I'll go and not return … when death has closed the door.
But God will open His door and I will enter in,
I won't turn back and I won't look back … I will forever be with Him.
But if you go your own way, you'll miss His loving care,
The quiet place you would have had … the burdens He would bear.
Don't forget with every choice, God is testing you,
To see if you will trust in Him with everything you do.
Put your trust in Jesus and find the peace you're searching for,
And when your life comes to an end, you'll walk through Heaven's door.
It's our destination wedding and as we gather around the throne,
We realize that we're the bride and Heaven's our new home.

The Real Deal

You need to go to Wesco to get your gas. It's a little out of your way,
    but it's
two cents less.
And if you go to Sam's Club and buy the big TV; you get $10 bucks
    off and the
second one's free.
Now everyone's talking about all the deals around. But no one's
    talking about
the best deal in town.
Because when you go to Calvary, He'll take your guilt and shame.
And if you go, one thing you'll know … you won't come back like
    you came.
Jesus is the Real Deal and He has some specials, too.
He'll save your soul and make you whole … to mention just a few.
So if you hear Him knocking, you need to let Him in.
If you harden your heart, He might depart and not be back again.
So if you hear Him knocking, just open up the door, you're going to
    find the kind
of deal your heart's been searching for.

I Need You

Lord, I need you even now before I start my day … to fill my heart and fill my
mind with only you, I pray.
A prayer like this I realize the world won't understand, but all my hopes and all
my dreams I know come from your hand.
And as I go throughout my day, I'll need you even more; to sort and pick through
things I do so I can spend more time with you.
When the world keeps trying to choke you out, when it fills my head with fear
and doubt.
That's when I'm going to need you more, only You can make my spirit soar.
It's a wonder how you hide yourself from those that don't know You.
Your glory fills all the earth; it fills the heavens, too.
It fills the seas and fills the land; every breath we have comes from Him.
But yet You make the blind to see; with eyes of faith they, too, believe.
So the blind can see, and the deaf have heard, what an awesome, amazing God
we serve!

Don't Miss Eternity

Satan is your enemy. Let's talk about him.
If you don't know your enemy, every battle he will win.
This is a strategy used in war, and you're at war, you see.
You should be concerned about this war; it involves your eternity.
I'm going to be very honest and make this very clear.
If you're not serving God, who are you serving down here?
You can only serve one master, and he will determine your destiny.
If you're not serving God, it will be hot in your eternity.
In life, if you've been drinking, good friends will take your key.
But with God, if you're not thinking, you could miss eternity.
Now you must really think this through. I've made my choice, this
    one's for you.
Some don't believe in the devil and that's his master plan.
He's already won the battle and you didn't even raise a hand.
The devil's like a lion that's prowling for his prey.
If you don't see him coming, his supper's on the way.
It could be life up till now has just been a breeze, but maybe it's time that
someone took away your keys.

Taking Out the Trash

Do you only go to God when there's nowhere else to go? Is He like last on your list of people that need to know?

Or maybe you just dump on Him … unload all your trash. You give Him all your rotten stuff, the things you know won't last.

Now people like that can really get you down, so you need to just excuse yourself when these people come around.

God knows all of our troubles that we bring to Him each day. But what really makes Him happy is when we praise Him anyway.

He is very patient and His compassion has no end. So if you want to make His day, begin to worship Him.

No matter how you're feeling or what you're going through, if you praise Him in everything, He'll want to be with you.

So praise Him in the morning before you start your day; before you're up and running, take some time to stop and pray.

If you walk with Him, He'll walk with you … If you talk with Him, He'll talk with you, too.

A grateful heart is what God needs … it's like honey to the bees. So if you've been complaining that God just can't be found, maybe you need to keep a little honey around.

The next time you complain about what people put you through …

Maybe you should ask yourself … have I been dumping on God too?

Final Notice

What an incredible story with an incredible plan! God designed it all from beginning to end.

His ways are not our ways … He knows what will be. From the first to the last, all things He can see.

His thoughts are much higher and wiser than ours. With the breath of His mouth, He created the stars.

We fell from His grace on the day Adam sinned. He was living in Paradise and walking with Him.

But God in His wisdom did think all things through. He knew we would fall and He knew what to do.

He would put on our flesh … this was His plan. And become one of us to redeem all of man.

Since the beginning of time, God sets the scene. He's the Alpha and Omega and all things in between.

There is none like Him … if you search, you will see. He was and He is and He always will be.

Do you know who put the stars in the sky? Because there's a time to be born and a time you must die.

Are you ready today if you took your last breath? Do you know where you'll go from the grave after death?

This is my job … to warn you, my friend. I've been called by the Lord, an ambassador of Him.

If I do not tell you, your blood is on me. But if you do not listen, a fool you will be.

A Letter to a Friend

I guess I better warn you so I can say I told you so; there is a God, the Bible's true, and you will be judged on what you know.

I can tell you Bible stories … you could even shed a tear. But if Jesus is not your savior, it works against you up there.

Some have never heard the truth … that Jesus can save them from their sin. But if you heard and don't believe, your judgment's worse than them.

Jesus said this will judge us starting at His Word, so you're better off on Judgment Day if you really never heard.

It's not true for those who love Him and want to call Him Lord. But those that don't … the Word of God is sharper than a sword.

One day, it will expose the way you really feel about Him. I hope you're comfortable in your own shoes … I know that I sure am.

The Word of God is powerful … it can break down Satan's lies. So I'm praying for you that one day soon, it will open up your eyes.

I'm sending you this letter … my intent is not in vain. My hope for you is one day soon, you'll call on Jesus's name.

I can't bear the thought that in Heaven you won't be there, so I'm on my knees praying for you that Heaven we both can share.

Now, don't send me an IOU … your debt's already been paid. Jesus paid it on the cross, then rose up from the grave.

I hope you get this letter in time….I tried to rush it through. And when you do, remember this … I'm still praying for you.

What Side of the Fence Are You On?

When God's living in you, that's a majority you see.
You can be way outnumbered and still watch your enemy flee.
But if there's idols in your heart, and your enemy's chasing you.
He'll steal your blessings one by one and there's nothing you can do.
I'll tell you now … you should beware … you're no match for him.
If God's not living in you, this enemy will win.
A blessing or a curse … you need to choose between the two.
You can't just stay on the fence when the devil's chasing you.
But as for me and my house, we will choose the Lord.
I want God's blessings to follow me and live forevermore.
One thing always happens when Jesus is around.
God's blessings overtake us and the curse cannot be found.
The choice is very simple, but I will make it really clear.
Fear and death on that side … peace and blessings here.
So if you're searching for God's blessings, I can tell you the way.
Jesus is the way … He's all you need today.
And now if you're still wondering what side you need to choose,
I would probably choose the side you can't afford to lose.

The Sinner's Prayer

I hope we all get to heaven, but God's Word is pretty clear. Some will miss by eighteen inches between their heart and their ear.

Oh, I know they will say we're hypocrites and guess what, it's probably true; but we found grace, and we found mercy … I pray to God you find it too.

Are we really hypocrites? Now you could make the case. Because we mess up now and then, we're known to make mistakes.

But when we fall down, we get up again. We learn, we grow, we follow Him. It's what you don't know I really fear. Because our eyes can see and our ears can hear.

I don't know how, but I remember when I prayed the sinner's prayer to Him. So, God, to you my prayer will be, you'll open their eyes so they can see.

So if you want you can pray with me, "Lord Jesus, I've sinned and I've lost my way. I forgot your cross and the price you paid.

I have nothing to offer and nothing to give; I cry out for your mercy and my sins to forgive."

Now if you really meant that prayer, there's a party in heaven with angels there.

They're singing and dancing around God's throne, because one more child of His went home.

But there's one more thing that you must do to seal your faith and prove it's true … go tell someone what God has done. You once were blind but now you see.

You don't know how, but you remember when you prayed a sinner's prayer to Him.

Living for Jesus Is Not Part-time Volunteer

You say you're following Jesus now; you said a prayer, you vowed a vow.
"Well, I'm sure glad I got that done." No, you're not done; you've just begun.
Because your flesh isn't dead until it dies. It'll raise its head ... don't be surprised.
You can't talk your old talk and walk your new walk. You have to watch the
things you do and say. Your words will judge you on Judgment Day.
I'm not trying to discourage you, but I need to be clear; Because living for
Jesus, it's not part-time volunteer. He's more than worth all your heart, so you
need to make sure you get a good start. Did you really, really see your sin? Did
you ever cry out, "Oh, wretched man that I am." I just want to make sure what
you have is real, you could easily miss Jesus if you go by what you feel.
The friends you made along life's way; some will go and some will stay.
Your old man must die to sin, not just once but again and again.
When you've been born again, it's easy to do, that's because Jesus is living in
you. If you're not born again, you'll surely fail, your new man will fall and your
old man prevail. I hope this message makes it clear, that living for Jesus is not
part-time volunteer.

How Big Is Your God?

You say your God, he's really cool. He lets you swear and bend the rules.
And go to church … that's not for me. I can watch those preachers
on TV.
So you think your God is a lot more fun because the God you serve
makes you
number 1.
Now the God of the Bible would never agree. Because the God you
serve is
no bigger than me.
So if you are the God of all that you do; that would make your God
no bigger
than you.
Now to make us happy that's not His plan. But to make us holy so
we look
more like Him.
Look up to the Heavens … now what do you see? Because your
God's too small,
you must agree.
You have your opinion; I also have mine. But when it comes to
God's Word,
he draws the line.
So what makes you think you are happier than me? I might have
something that you cannot see.
Because deep in your heart, there's a place you can't fill. You've tried
it with
things, but it's emptier still.
You wonder sometimes why you feel so alone? That place in your
heart can
be only God's home.

Is Your God Too Small?

God always was and always will be; you don't carve Him from a tree
He's in control of everything … without Him nothing would exist.
God would never say, "Oops, I didn't see that!" There's nothing He
    would miss.
He knows the thoughts that are in your head; they are not hidden
    from Him.
Everything that was and everything that will be from beginning to
    the end.
He's also a lot smarter than we could ever be;
It only took the breath of God to create you and me.
He made his glory known when He revealed to us his Son.
All the Godhead dwells in him … he is the Three in One.
There is no valley low enough that you can't find Him there.
The highest mountain … it's not too high … you see He's everywhere.
God would never create a universe that was bigger than Him;
So forget how big you thought God was … you need to think again.
When you look up into the heavens thousands of light-years away,
Don't forget God's bigger yet … He's all you'll need today.

Lord, Go Deeper

Are your motives pure? Is your heart true? Because God, who is
    all-knowing,
can see right through.
This is the place where I'm tested the most. Because deep in my heart
    are my
motives exposed.
When you hear yourself saying, "Lord, it's not fair," let God go deeper
    to see
what's down there.
Sometimes the things that irritate you might be just a sign of what
    God's trying to do.
So instead of resisting and say it's not fair, let God go deeper to see
    what's
down there.
Search us, Oh Lord, and help us to see. No matter how painful or
    hard it will be.
You alone can help us to heal, when You take out the hurt and the
    pain that we feel.
We'll sing Your praises when You are through, because the freer we
    are when we're trusting in You.
So the next time you're hurt or filled with despair, you might hear
    God saying, "I'm working down here."

Finding the Lord

Are you finding the Lord in your own heart in your own mind?
Are you finding the Lord in your own thoughts in your own time?
I used to think the Lord was a big step for me, but I took that step
And searched for Him and found out differently.
I thought God's love was far away like a star up in the sky;
But when I went to reach for him, He came down by my side.
When we get lost, God's love is there, but like sheep, we go astray.
Don't be afraid, just take His hand; the shepherd knows the way.
Let His love be like the snow that falls upon the earth.
Make it stay so it can grow, then let it melt so it can flow.
Have you ever seen a morning sun that takes the night away,
And as it brightens up the sky did you ever wonder, did you won-
    der why?
I've often thought, "How can this be," then I found Him and now I see.
I found God through His word and through all His precious people
Who brought me to the one I love then set me free that I could see
That Christ had really died for me. He died for me.

Will You Be With Jesus?

When I get to Heaven and when I'm finally home, I'll be glad to see my loved ones ... but I'm headed for the throne.

I know there's lots of angels there and exciting things to see, but when I arrive in Heaven, there's one place I need to be.

This could sound a little selfish, but I want some time with Him; He's helped me through so many things and become my closest friend.

He found me when I was broken and had no hope inside. He breathed in me the breath of life and my spirit came alive.

So you see why I must find Him ... even if I have to wait. I won't be in a hurry there ... if I'm beyond the pearly gate.

He might come out to greet me when I get near His throne. I'll run into His arms, I know ... as He tells me, "Welcome home."

So many things to thank Him for ... where will I begin? I'll probably forget every word when I take one look at Him!

Lord, it's been a long journey, but now I'm finally home; could I just stay with You awhile ... right here by your throne?

Now you know I'm only dreaming, but one day it will be true. Do you have dreams of Heaven? I surely hope you do.

And do you know this Jesus ... has He become your friend? Because if He's not, you need to know you might not be with Him.

God Was in This Storm

I'm out on the water, Lord, but I can't swim or float. If it wasn't You
that called me out, I'm getting back into that boat.

This water, Lord, is over my head. Was that You calling me? I've gone
too far to turn back now … the boat I cannot see.

Others that were in the boat, they said I wouldn't dare. But I stepped
out; where are You, Lord? I really need you here.

This water's deep and my faith is small … Lord, what will I do? I
could try to swim to shore, but I would rather trust in You.

I know I have your seed of faith You put inside of me. But if it doesn't
grow right now, I'll be carried out to sea.

How small or big this storm really is, I surely do not know. But if I
didn't get out of that boat, my faith would never grow.

I would like to tell you my faith stood strong until I passed this test.
But the storm raged on … where are you, Lord? When will my
soul find rest?

Now at last the storm has passed … the sun is breaking through.
Lord, I thought I was all alone but the storm was really You.

God tries our hearts in the storms of life, so put your trust in Him. Get
out of the boat, let faith arise … He'll teach you how to swim.

What's Precious to You?

If your life down here has left you needy, I know the solution … you need to get greedy.

Yep, that's what I said … get greedy, my friend. But be greedy for Jesus…now your needs won't just end.

One thing will happen as you go through your day; The things that you needed one by one go away.

He supplies all of our needs … I found this to be. When I'm greedy for Jesus, He satisfies me.

So forget the big boat or that house on the hill. And get greedy for Jesus … you might get them still.

Because the things of this world are not precious, you see. Not like loved ones and friendships or your own family.

But mostly love Jesus, who's more precious than all. And the things of this world will look pretty small.

Don't be like the dog that kept chasing his tail. He's accomplishing nothing even if he prevails.

Remember, Oh Lord, that we are but dust. Who else can we turn to if You don't help us?

When the world looks too big and You look too small, remind us again who created it all.

Are You Wise?

Get wisdom in this life no matter what you do. Don't live for gold or silver ... only wisdom stays with you.

Wisdom knows there is a God and Jesus His only Son. And every knee one day will bow before His kingdom comes.

Do you know the first commandment? Well, this is how it goes ... You are to love the Lord your God with all your heart and soul.

God is not a puppy or a fuzzy teddy bear ... The beginning of wisdom is to fear Him; do you need some balance there?

So if you want to go to heaven, this is my advice. Read His word; pray to Him ... don't just roll the dice.

I know that everyone says we are going to a better place. But did you know God's Word is clear ... most will miss His grace.

Take your gold and silver ... go out and have your fun. Ninety years you might have, but eternity's just begun.

So what would it profit you if you had all the world's gold, but lost your soul for eternity where there's riches yet untold.

The things you see are temporary ... the things you don't see forever. By faith, we believe every word of God because He can lie ... no, never.

So let's conclude this matter ... stay with me now I pray. If you want to be in heaven, make sure you're saved today.

Are You Searching?

Are you tired of wondering what life's all about? I mean why are you
here … have you figured it out?

Maybe you're chasing all the dreams from within, to find when you
have them, you're empty again.

Have you ever considered something new in your life? It's not a new
husband, a house, or a wife.

The things of this world are not going to do. You'll find when you
have them, sometimes they have you.

Will you spend your whole life to come to the end and take a look
back and be empty again?

Are you ready right now to figure this out? To find out what life is
really about.

If you're searching for something to satisfy you, then God is the One
that you should look to.

He will fill every need that your heart's longing for, then fill it again …
then a little bit more.

Till you're overflowing with His blessings from above … you'll stand
back amazed at His incredible love.

You can spend your life searching, but your searching is in vain. You'll
never find fulfillment even close to the same.

Take my word, now I'll say it again … He'll fill you much fuller than
you've ever been.

Jesus Is Our Lighthouse

Here's a story of a navy destroyer that ruled over sea and land. No plane or boat could veer its course … he would move for none of them.

With its guided missiles fully loaded to go, he alone controlled the sea. Everyone who picked a fight with him was now just a memory.

The captain himself was a man of war, the ocean was his to cruise. If you picked a fight with this destroyer, it was you to be sure to lose.

On the horizon, there's a light in the distance … the first mate would call ahead.

"Move your course five degrees to the right."

"No, You must move instead."

The captain was furious as he grabbed the mike, "My guns are aimed at you.

Move your course five degrees to the right, or you will see what they can do."

"I am Private First Class John Smith, you must give me room."

"I'm the captain of a navy destroyer, turn or meet your doom."

A voice called back, "You can never move me, my foundation is on a rock. I am a lighthouse for all to see and come safely to my dock.

There only one route I will let you take. Now you will listen to me. Turn your course five degrees to the right and head back out to sea."

The Captain was silent as he veered his course … something he had never done.

He had fought many battles and won many wars, but this Private First Class had won.

Jesus is our lighthouse … His word is ever true. When the destroyer comes with his big guns, He will fight for you.

So turn your course if you don't know him, the cross is solid ground. Don't build your house on sinking sand when the Destroyer is still around.

Get Out of the Water ... NOW!

I had no idea when I answered His call, that the life I was living had no profit at all.

But little by little and line upon line, He would teach me His ways one day at a time.

So don't be surprised when you look in the mirror ... Your old man must die and your new man appear.

Had I known all this and could do it again ... I would start even sooner than I did back then.

The sooner you find Him, the better you'll be. You could miss today's blessing God wants you to see.

Satan will keep you as long as he can because he knows when you find Jesus, his power will end.

But each day you wait and every hour that goes by, his grip just gets tighter; if you're believing his lie.

Remember, he's a deceiver ... he'll keep you in sin and tell you, "This Jesus, you'll do fine without Him."

Don't be like the frog in a pan of hot water. Jump out now before the pan just gets hotter.

The longer you wait, the harder it will be. Then Satan will laugh when hell's fire you see.

Are You Winning the Battle?

So what's your purpose in life … your goals and your dreams? Is God in your thoughts or is your mind filled with things?

Is your to-do list so long that for God there's no time? Are the toys on your shelf all stuck in your mind?

Examine your heart … is that something you do? So the things that you have don't really have you.

Our hearts are a gift that we give to God; because above all things, He wants our love.

Are you willing right now to examine your heart and to take out the things that keep you apart?

If you listen close, you can hear God say, "Leave room in your heart for Me today."

There's a battle going on and you're in it to; it's not over money or land … it's for you.

Our commander is Jesus … He knows the way. He's been here before … He can help you today.

Our hearts are the treasure that we're fighting for because who has your heart will win this war.

If you're trusting Jesus, this battle you'll win. Don't trust in your flesh … it will deceive you, my friend.

"If it feels good, just do it" will lead you astray, and the cross you once cherished will get in your way.

Sin's fun for a season … we all will agree. But the cross will bring joy for all eternity.

Are You Special?

Once upon a time, there were four little girls who grew up in a very loving home.

Their father would tell them that you are the special one, the most precious are you alone.

One day, the girls were all out to play, that's when the youngest one said, "Father told me that I was the special one." The others all shook their head.

So the secret was out what the father had done … he made them all special … yes, every one.

That's so like what our heavenly father would do when he tells us there's none quite as special as you.

Not one of us alike and never again, but we're only special if we're living for him.

One day, he'll show us how special we are … when he was nailed to that cross, every nail left a scar.

When we're with him in Heaven, all his glory we'll see, even the scars left for you and for me.

We become special when we call on his name. He made us all special, but we're all not the same.

So if you want to be special, now you know what to do … put your trust in Jesus …

He'll make you special, too.

Not Just a Fairy Tale

Make sure you don't miss heaven … are you on His path today? So many paths to choose from, but only one's the narrow way.

Don't be left behind … one day that trumpet's going to sound. Only those that took the narrow path will be heaven-bound.

You've been invited to a wedding, but reservations are required. If your name is in the Book of Life, your ticket's been acquired.

This trip will be fast … in just a twinkling of the eye. We'll make one stop along the way to meet up in the sky.

Hey, we're going to a banquet … there's a wedding going on. Forget the stuff you have down here … you won't need it if you're gone.

What's neat about this wedding … we all get to be His bride. And one by one, He'll call our name and usher us inside.

So are you watching and waiting to hear that trumpet sound? The dead in Christ will hear it first and come up from the ground.

And we, if we're still living, will join them in the sky. And be with Him forevermore … in that sweet by and by.

You will see old friends and loved ones that He raised up from their tombs. But most of all, we'll see Jesus … we're His bride and He's our groom.

I'll see Moses and Abraham and lots of angels too. But one more thing I hope to see … I hope to be seeing you.

One More Story

With all the noise and clamber that runs through your head, do you ever sit still and listen, instead?

I mean really listen, but not with your ear; there's things going on … if you're quiet, you'll hear.

I'm not talking about Yoga or how to find your inner man. This is hard to explain … just come with me if you can.

We'll make a stop along the way and visit with Despair. If you get close, you'll hear him say, "I should have listened way back there."

And what about him … can you see him yet? I see him everywhere … his name is Regret.

We need to visit this little church I like to call my home. It's a good place to finish up and try to end this poem.

Over there is Sally … she was with Pride. Someone told her about Jesus. She believed and came inside.

And this is Jack … he hung out with Despair. But he asked Jesus in his heart, and now he's coming here.

I could go on and on … Jesus is calling many home, but the one I'm really looking for is the one who reads this poem.

No Regrets

I have no regrets and I need to thank You,
Because You have healed all the hurts in my life I've been through.
If I could do life all over again, I wouldn't change one thing I did
    back then.
You have carefully gone through and healed my deepest pain.
Turned them around and only You would use them for my gain.
All the things in life that really hurt me so …
It was You that had the plans that would one day make me whole.
Now to all those that are wondering if God's word is faithful and true;
I have no regrets … remember that … and I pray the same for you.
Too many people in this world die with such regrets.
If Jesus would have been their Lord, we know that death is better yet.
On that day when angels come to carry me away,
I want the things I did down here to continue on, I pray.
I would like people to say of me … my work down here was through.
He didn't leave one thing undone … that's why I'm home with You.
So come to Him just as you are and your new legacy will be …
He lived his life with no regrets since Jesus set him free.

I Dare You

Will you pray to God today? You don't have to speak … He knows
your thoughts and everything you say.

Have you ever done something on a dare? Then I dare you now to
take a stand and pray a simple prayer.

God searches the world looking for someone who will pray to Him.
Maybe today, He'll find you … I dare you once again.

If you're reading this poem, take time for Him today. It would take
just a little prayer for God to look your way.

I could beg or I could plead, but you're the one who has the need.
Think about it, if you really want to, but is it wrong to pray to
the One who made you?

You have a free will no matter what I say, but if I was you, I would
stop and pray today.

Now Satan might tell you you're not good enough, my friend. Don't
listen to that liar, he's the master of all sin.

Of course, we're not good enough … that's why Jesus died for us. Our
righteousness is like filthy rags, but He nailed them to His cross.

So if your life is like a tumble weed blowing in the wind; why don't
you pray to Jesus now … I dare you once again.

Lord Jesus, I've sinned and I've lost my way. I've forgotten your cross
and the price You paid. I have nothing to offer and nothing to
give … I cry out for your mercy and my sins to forgive. Now
if you really meant that prayer, there's a party in heaven with
angels there. They're singing and dancing around God's throne
because one more child of His went home. But there's one more
thing that you must do, to seal your faith and prove it's true.
Go tell someone what God has done you once were blind, but
now you see you don't know how but you remember when, you
dared to pray this prayer to him.

About the Author

I was raised in a home where reading the Bible was just for pastors or priests, and we are now seeing the effects of it. As churches are closing their doors every day, the church is getting smaller and God is no longer politically correct in our schools. We have raised a generation of children that are walking away from their faith, but God is raising up an army of young people who are loving him in a way that he has always wanted to be loved. As the church cries out for this next generation, we need to introduce our children to the real Jesus …a Jesus who listens, cares and wants to be a big part of their lives. So when our enemy comes at them like a lion, they will be filled with the truth and overcome him. I love the stories of Noah and the Ark, David and Goliath, Joshua and the walls of Jericho, but I think a better story is when our children tell us about what God is doing in their lives today.

Please contact author at: twchristianpoems@outlook.com

CPSIA information can be obtained
at www.ICGtesting.com
Printed in the USA
FSHW020402120720
71675FS